THE EFFLUENT SOCIETY

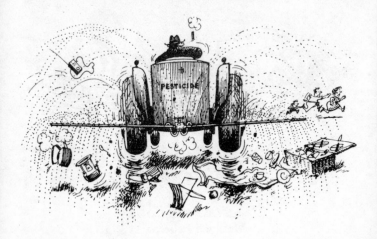

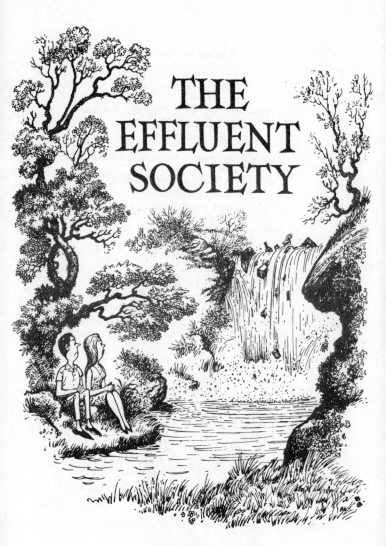

THE EFFLUENT SOCIETY

MAGNUM BOOKS
Methuen Paperbacks Ltd

A Magnum Book

THE EFFLUENT SOCIETY
ISBN 0 417 01050 8

First published 1971 by Methuen & Co. Ltd
Magnum edition published 1978 .
Reprinted 1978

Copyright © 1971 by Norman Thelwell

Magnum Books are published by
Methuen Paperbacks Ltd
11 New Fetter Lane, London EC4 4EE

Made and printed in Great Britain by
Richard Clay (The Chaucer Press) Ltd
Bungay, Suffolk

*Most of the cartoons in this book originally
appeared in* Punch *and are reproduced by
permission of the proprietors*

CONTENTS

"I'm glad you won't be needing the kiss of life!"

WATER, WATER EVERYWHERE

"They'll have to do something soon. It's affecting polar bears in the Arctic."

"Only *you* could get becalmed in sewage."

"Hello! We can't be far from civilisation."

"False alarm! It's untreated sewage."

"Watch where you're sitting. There's detergent all over the place."

"We're very lucky here. The sewage forms a barrier that no oil can get through."

"It may not do the river much good but it brings up my whites a treat."

"The biological action has digested your socks."

"You can catch them ready cooked down by the power station!"

"I daren't go in. The chlorine dries my skin up."

"Have you been spraying your roses again?"

"I liked it better before they put Fluoride in it."

THE GOOD EARTH

"Trust *you* to tread in some chemical or other."

"These damned chemical sprays are a menace."

"You *enjoy* raping the English countryside don't you?"

"Hello! They're nibbling at the green belt again."

"The trouble is, you can't see the trees for wood."

"Suppose we all decided to take one home for Christmas—*then* what?"

"We're very lucky, when you think about it,
working in such beautiful surroundings."

A BREATH OF FRESH AIR

"Mind if I smoke?"

"I should put that fag out.
I'm sure I can smell gas."

"Every man for himself! We've struck nerve-gas."

"It's no use carrying on like that Dad! Atmospheric pollution's at an acceptable level."

"Loosen the stopper."

DOWN IN THE DUMPS

"It's astonishing how personal possessions accumulate."

"It's a scheme of great boldness and vision. They're ploughing the whole place up for wheat."

"I'm worried about Charlie.
The boot hasn't been slept in."

"Don't ring the police! I think it's the one
we dumped near St. Albans."

"I wondered when the country folk
would start to retaliate."

THE RACE FOR SPACE

"There's talk of trying to acquire it for the nation!"

"On balance, it might be better to do our motoring during the day and sail at night."

"It's nature's way of keeping down the numbers."

"Right. Last one in is a sissy!"

"Ask them to move back—and hurry!"

"Look right, look left . . ."

"How do they find their own nests?"

ANIMAL FARM

"Run along and help Grandad freeze the chickens!"

"We're having trouble with foxes."

"He makes sure his *own* Christmas dinner
has a bit of flavour."

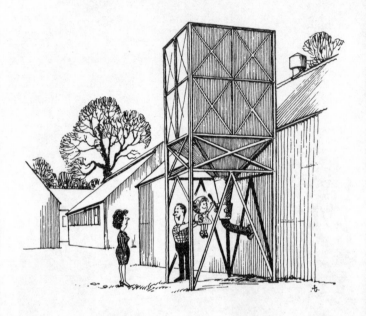

"She loves feeding the animals."

"You don't care a damn what I look like."

"I'll clear the way to the bar—
you get the beer."

"I'm moving the turkeys to the
maximum security block."

"Hold it, Simpson! He's a trusty."

"Nobody will ever build on this land
while I'm farming it."

". . . and it's *so* kind to my hands."

"There are two tons of cattle-cake to come."

"This is our new improved potato harvester—
unless I'm very much mistaken."

RHUBARB!

"I can remember the days when haystacks
were comfortable."

ALL CREATURES GREAT
AND SMALL

"For heaven's sake be careful! Remember they're rare."

"Don't be hysterical! They've got as much right to live as we have."

"It's no good being sentimental. They've got to be thinned out."

"By the time you've got all the oil off them, you've got to retrain them to dive for fish."

"Over my dead body!
There's a robin nesting in the sump."

"Don't hurt him!"

"Go on! Swipe them.
There's no one looking."

"Get ready! They'll run for it any minute now."

"I'm afraid it will mean destroying
their natural habitat."

"So far I've spotted thirteen hedgehogs, four rabbits, a squirrel, three rooks, a chaffinch and a pied wagtail."

"Relax—it's one of ours."

"No! No! She fended him off again. . . .
Now he's gone to sleep."

"If these Antarctic holiday tours catch on,
this place is going to look like
Blackpool beach in a few years time."

"It's good television! But is it good colour television?"

"Winter's over!"

"I prefer to have green-fly
and a clear conscience."

"He did great work for the preservation of wild life."

TECHNICAL HITCH

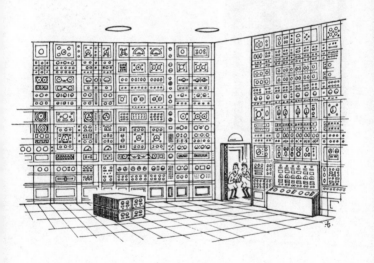

"My God, Simpson! That wasn't there when we locked up."

"You're *bound* to feel nervous
the first time on television."

"Cut them out and transplant them.
That's my advice."

"I'll swap you two kidneys for it."

"Oh well, there goes another three million quids worth of research."

"A blasted power-cut, just as I was cleaning my teeth."

"Run for it. The water main's burst."

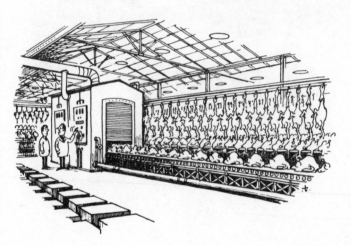

"This is a miracle of modern science. It puts in flavour."

"Quiet, it's Charlie. They've made
another gas strike."

"According to statistics—she's the coldest
secretary we've had since February,
nineteen forty six."

COMPUTED WEDLOCK

"According to our computer, Mr. Pearson . . ."

"I'll never
understand what that stupid machine **saw in** you."

"I knew there'd be a snag—
he thinks I'm a machine."

"I never programmed for her mother."

"It picks couples with identical interests. We're both interested in a divorce."

THE GRAVE NEW WORLD

'It's an oblong piece, with a window
and a bit of balcony."

"Do you mind turning down the volume?"

"You'd better get washed and changed.
They're having company."

"There are a lot of milk bottles. Do you think we
should check that they're all right?"

"I'm sorry! I'm a stranger round here myself."

"Hello! The vandals have been in again."

"The story goes that the place was
once used by smuggl . . ."

"It needs adjusting. They should go blue
when they're strangled."

"Sex and violence! It's all we ever get."

"The church must move with the times brothers—
we're going into the after-shave business."

LET'S PROTEST

"Which embassy's this?"

"It's that crowd from the agricultural college."

"We might as well face it J.B. There's an atmosphere of unrest among the workers."

"I don't think it's anything intellectual, dear—
they're from the university."

"I've always contended that there are *some*
decent youngsters about."

"He's asked for political asylum."

"I understand it was caused by an off-side
decision at White Hart Lane."

"Call yourself a supporter?"

"All the same—I agree with
what he said to the ref."